Hope for the Future

Devotional Poems
written and illustrated
by B. Kaye Jones

Kevin
Mayhew

First published in Great Britain in 1996 by
KEVIN MAYHEW LTD
Rattlesden
Bury St Edmunds
Suffolk IP30 0SZ

ISBN 0 86209 835 1
Catalogue No 1500050

Typesetting by Louise Hill
Printed in Hong Kong

CONTENTS

FOREWORD

This is now my third book, and if you have read my first two, *Just for Today*, then *Strength for Tomorrow*, you will be able to trace the dealings of God in my life; from the shock and pain of first having cancer, through a recurrence of the disease and further surgery, to the present time, when I have come to terms, by the grace of God, with what has been happening to me, and beginning to see the fruit that comes from suffering – that it hasn't been in vain.

These little books are a direct fruit of this trial; I do not think they would have ever been published when I was healthy, and busy in the Lord's work – so God's 'full-stop' in my life was to re-direct me, amongst other reasons, to something else he had planned for my life.

I hope this will encourage others who have been laid aside, or stopped in some way – it can seem so purposeless, but it isn't so – God always wants to do something more in our hearts, in our characters and in our lives – the 'pruning' of God, that we bear more fruit.

Though painful, it is worth it all, and we are never quite the same again.

I would take this opportunity to thank my wonderful husband and dear family for the love and support I have received from them, along with those praying friends who were of the 'Barnabas' type – sons of consolation!

'Now may our Lord Jesus Christ himself, and our God and Father, who has loved us and given us everlasting consolation and good hope by grace, comfort your hearts.' (2 THESSALONIANS 2:16-17)

B. KAYE JONES

Faith, Hope and Love

May hope be the source of all my comfort, all my joy;
and faith my spirit's strength, my victor's song;
let love be the motivating force of all I do –
the love of Christ, eternal, true and strong.

And now abideth faith, hope and love, these three;
but the greatest of these is love.

1 Cor. 13:13

THE POTTER

It was marred in the hand of the potter –
my vessel was flawed on the wheel;
broken down, then re-formed to his pattern,
so the clay bears the print of his seal.

*The vessel that he made of clay was marred in the hand
of the potter; so he made it again into another vessel,
as it seemed good to the potter to make.*

JEREMIAH 18:4

THE CRUCIBLE

In this furnace I can feel you changing me –
I will never be the same again;
purifying fire, your heat refining me
so that gold is fashioned from my pain.

… that the genuineness of your faith, being much more
precious than gold that perishes, though it is tested by fire,
may be found to praise, honour and glory at
the revelation of Jesus Christ.

1 PETER 1:7

Brave Heart

(a tribute to Joanne Gillespie,
writer of two best-sellers,
who died of cancer aged 15)

She wrote to me when I was down
and at my lowest ebb,
a bright and cheery little note:
'have faith in God' it said.
My mind was filled with gloomy thoughts,
my soul, with dread and fear,
her hopeful words were comforting,
and somehow God seemed near.
She lightened many darkened lives –
a candle burning bright;
and now she shines forever blessed
in heaven's greater light.

*And there shall be no night there: they need no lamp nor
light of the sun, for the Lord God gives them light.
And they shall reign forever and ever.*

REVELATION 22:5

LISTENING

In a quiet, secret place
someone waits to see your face –
to know you listen;
someone longs to speak to you,
bring his peace like morning dew –
O, won't you listen?

In his love he waits for you,
asking, do you love him too –
enough to listen?
Turn your eyes upon his face,
he will give you power and grace –
when you listen.

O my dove, in the clefts of the rock,
in the secret places of the cliff,
let me see your countenance,
let me hear your voice;
for your voice is sweet,
and your countenance is lovely.

SONG OF SOLOMON 2:14

FAITHFUL GOD

I come and fall before you
to worship and adore you
and give to you the praise due to your name;
most holy God, Jehovah,
Redeemer, mighty Saviour,
our faithful God, forever you're the same.

You, O Lord, are our Father;
our Redeemer from Everlasting is your name.

ISAIAH 63:16

LET GO

He loves you when you feel you cannot love yourself,
when bitter thoughts possess your mind;
he loves you with a heart of tenderness and hope,
let go – and leave it all behind.

*… let us lay aside every weight, and the sin which so
easily ensnares us, and let us run with endurance the
race that is set before us, looking unto Jesus …*

HEBREWS 12:1-2

He Cares

God is here, yes he is, and he loves you
though the shock, and the pain hide his face –
like a mist that has come down between you –
but he longs to give comfort and grace
for the trial that seems to engulf you,
and the grief that's too heavy to bear;
grasp the hand he is reaching down to you:
trust his love – you are safe in his care.

… I have loved you with an everlasting love;
therefore with loving kindness I have drawn you.

JEREMIAH 31:3

B Kaye Jones

17

TRUSTING

Is there a cross that is hard to endure,
or a burden too heavy to bear?
Lay all your cares at the feet of our Lord,
let them go – trust his love – leave them there.

Cast your burden on the Lord,
and he shall sustain you.

<small>PSALM 55:22</small>

TREASURES

Where is my treasure –
is it here, in my hands?
Do I value the things
such as houses or lands
and precious possessions,
or the things that I do
that please only myself,
and not done just for you?

Treasure in heaven –
is it there, where he is?
Hidden giving of self
with a love that is his;
a price that is costly
as the seed has to die –
to submit to his will
never questioning, 'why'?

These are the treasures
laid in heaven for me.
O, how poor they will seem
when his glory I see!

*Go your way, sell whatever you have and give to
the poor, and you will have treasure in heaven;
and come, take up the cross, and follow me.*

MARK 10:21

EMMAUS EXPERIENCE

Jesus will walk by my side –
when unbelief and disappointment hide
his face from view;
he'll be there to dispel the doubts and hurts, and in his
love, remind me of the blessings I once knew.

Jesus will walk by my side –
through mists of doubt the imprint in his hand,
I fail to see;
forgetting in my bitterness he suffered in my place,
he took my curse and pain to set me free.

Jesus will walk by my side –
the vale of tears, a living well he'll make unto my soul;
the desert place of unbelief will blossom once again,
as living waters cleanse and make me whole.

Jesus will walk by my side –
I feel a softening in my heart, that only he can bring;
the reservations fall away, I take again his hand
and joyfully my heart begins to sing.

Jesus will walk by my side –
He'll see me through, and when this flickering flame
of life grows dim;
the trials past, the joys, the tears are over, then I'll walk
for evermore, in paradise with him.

Jesus himself drew near and went with them.
But their eyes were restrained, so that they
did not know him.

LUKE 24:15-16

Causes

Does my Saviour really love me?
Have I sinned and grieved my Lord
that this illness should befall me –
were the warning signs ignored?
Yes, there were some needs and reasons
that were hidden deep within,
but the greatest 'cause' is glorious:
that my life bears fruit for him.

… and every branch that bears fruit he
prunes, that it may bear more fruit.

JOHN 15:2

RISE ABOVE IT

Disappointed, hurt, discouraged –
do you find your cup of trouble
full, right to the brim?
Don't go under, rise above it,
set your sights a little higher –
fix your eyes on him.

But my eyes are upon you, O God the Lord;
in you I take refuge; do not leave my soul destitute.

PSALM 141:8

*Make a joyful shout to God,
all the earth!*

PSALM 66:1

SPRING

There are primroses in the hollow,
sweetest clusters of palest gold;
there are soft, green buds on the hazel trees
and new-born lambs in the fold:
all nature around rejoices –
then why shouldn't my heart sing?
Songs of praise to our great Creator,
for the joy of new life – that is spring.

Sing out the honour of his name;
make his praise glorious.

PSALM 66:2

GOD'S HOLY LAMB

A babe was born at Bethlehem –
a child of joy, a child of woe;
a prince of peace, from heavenly throne
sent down to show God loves us so.

He made this sinful world his home –
a child of truth, a child of light;
a child to show the way to heaven,
a child of love, so pure and bright.

To save the souls of men from sin,
God's sinless child became a man;
a sacrifice to bleed and die –
this little child, God's holy lamb.

And so we sing this Christmas morn
a song of love, a song of joy,
a song of peace, a song of praise,
a carol to a baby boy.

For God so loved the world, that he gave his only begotten son, that whoever believes in him should not perish, but have everlasting life.

JOHN 3:16

His Answer

For the hurt of disappointment,
for the cynical and empty –
for the feelings of rejection and unworthiness;
for the bitterness of failure,
for the unforgiving nature,
there is an answer – God's faithfulness.

For your hurt, there is his healing,
for your shattered dreams – his heaven,
for your loneliness, his fellowship in all you do;
for your bitterness, his sweetness,
for your hardened heart, his mercy,
there is his answer – God's love for you.

… therefore I have hope …
because his compassions fail not.
They are new every morning:
great is your faithfulness.

Lamentations 3:21-23

The Lord will command his loving kindness in the daytime, and in the night his song shall be with me...

PSALM 42:7-8

MUSIC

If all the song of life was in a major key
how plain and tedious would my singing be;
the minor sound of black notes gives to me
a contrast, and a sweeter harmony.

Needless Fear

I was hanging suspended in space –
'don't look down!'
Nothing solid supporting my weight,
just a thread that was faith
that I clutched in my hands –
I just hung there, not knowing my fate;
so I waited in worry and fear –
'don't look down!'
Tense with panic, not making a sound,
then a voice spoke to me:
'don't be frightened, you're safe' –
I was hanging two feet above ground!

Are not two sparrows sold for a copper coin?
And not one of them falls to the ground apart from
your Father's will. Do not fear therefore;
you are of more value than many sparrows.

Matthew 10:29, 31

The White Rose

I hold in my hands a white rose –
plucked fresh from the garden this morn;
the sweet air is clean from the rain, and still
in the calm that comes following dawn.
His presence is all around me –
so awesome, I scarce understand
how I, God's fallen creation, can hold
the perfection of God in my hand.

You are worthy, O Lord, to receive glory,
honour and power; for you created all things,
and by your will they exist and were created.

REVELATION 4:11

EASTER SONG

Glorious morning,
new day is dawning,
gone from the tomb
Christ Jesus our Lord.
Death had enslaved us,
he died to save us,
rose from the grave
fulfilling his Word.

Christ has arisen–
wondrous new vision,
see him in splendour–
Christ glorified.
Hell could not hold him,
O, now behold him,
risen again our
Saviour who died.

Praises we bring him,
anthems we sing him,
crowned with great glory,
power and might.
Christ all-victorious,
vision all-glorious,
Christ resurrected
bursts on our sight.

… now Christ is risen from the dead.

1 Corinthians 15:20

ENGLAND

O England, our England –
a nation set apart
by truth and honour, motivating
men of valiant heart –
O England!

O England, our England –
who as a robe, once wore
integrity; the light of God
illuminating law –
O England!

O England, our England –
now other gods replace
our true God, who had made us once
a great and noble race –
O England!

O England, our England –
may once again be found
that Christian heritage, that made
our green and pleasant land –
Our England!

Righteousness exalts a nation,
but sin is a reproach to any people.

Prov. 14:34

Blessed is the nation whose God is the Lord.

Psalm 33:12

42

THE CROSS OF JESUS

Did someone reject and betray your love?
You pretended you did not care;
but at night, all alone, tears of grief were shed,
for the blow was too heavy to bear.
He gives us an answer to bitterness,
for the grief of a wounded soul –
at the foot of the cross we can find release:
by forgiving our hearts are made whole.

*And when they had come to the place called Calvary,
there they crucified him. Then said Jesus, 'Father,
forgive them, for they do not know what they do.'*

LUKE 23:33-34

Your Burden Laid Down

It's round the corner, out of sight, out of mind –
that ugly problem you have left behind;
and as a little child, you face today –
you choose to leave the past, to walk away
from fearful apprehensions; unbelief;
and trusting God, find solace and relief.

… let us lay aside every weight …

Hebrew 12:1

Cast your burden on the Lord,
and he shall sustain you ...

<small>Psalm 55:22</small>

Door of Hope

If something, somewhere in my words
has struck a chord, has touched your heart
with comfort, or has given hope in God,
then I have done my part –
however poor and small –
may 'Achor's troubled vale' become
a door of hope, that leads the way
to heaven, and you find your Saviour there;
then truly I can say –
I have fulfilled my call.

*I will give her … the valley of Achor [trouble]
as a door of hope; she shall sing there,
as in the days of her youth …*

Hosea 2:15